THE EUGÉNIE ROCHEROLLE SERIES

Intermediate Piano Solo

Mancini Classics

9 Piano Solos Arranged by Eugénie Rocherolle

ISBN 978-1-4803-4066-4

HAL•LEONARD®
CORPORATION

7777 W. BLUEMOUND RD. P.O. BOX 13819 MILWAUKEE, WI 53213

In Australia Contact:
Hal Leonard Australia Pty. Ltd.
4 Lentara Court
Cheltenham, Victoria, 3192 Australia
Email: ausadmin@halleonard.com.au

Visit Hal Leonard Online at
www.halleonard.com

For Justin

BABY ELEPHANT WALK
from the Paramount Picture HATARI!

By HENRY MANCINI
Arranged by Eugénie Rocherolle

Moderately fast (♩ = 120)

4

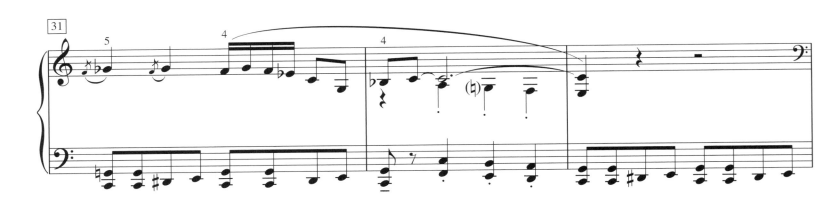

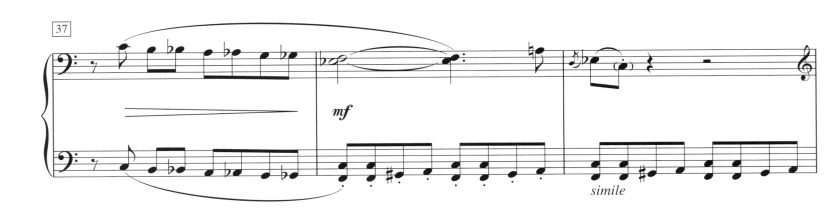

D.C. al Coda

CODA

cresc.

Slowly

CHARADE

from CHARADE

By HENRY MANCINI
Arranged by Eugénie Rocherolle

Moderate Waltz (♩ = 132)

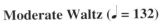

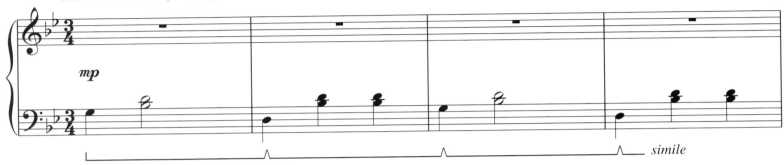

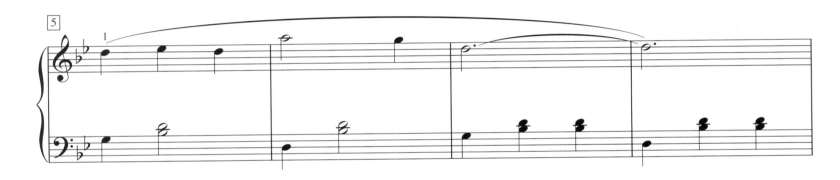

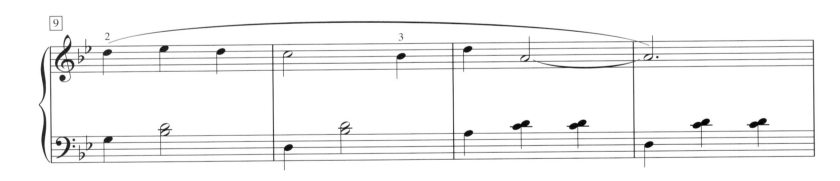

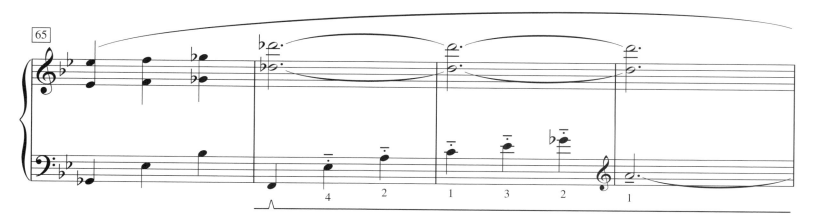

DAYS OF WINE AND ROSES

from DAYS OF WINE AND ROSES

Lyrics by JOHNNY MERCER
Music by HENRY MANCINI
Arranged by Eugénie Rocherolle

DEAR HEART

By HENRY MANCINI
Arranged by Eugénie Rocherolle

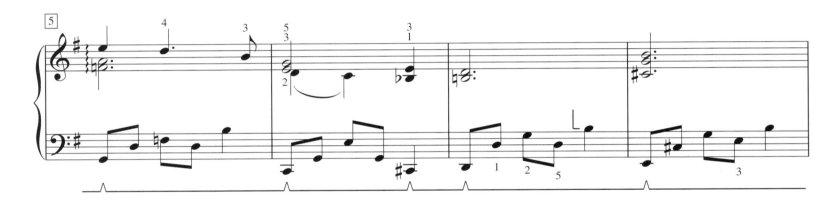

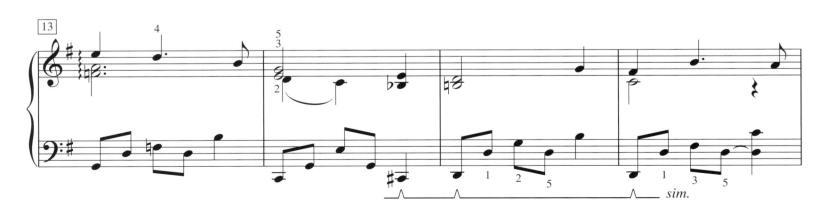

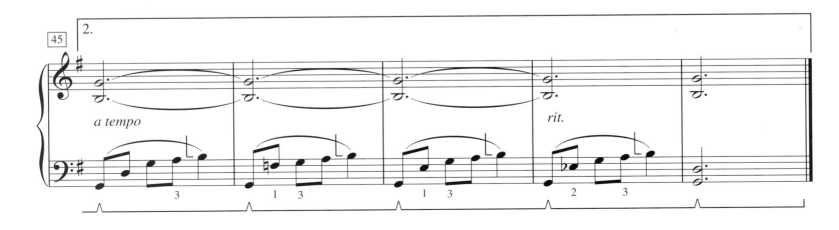

HOW SOON

Words by Al Stillman
Music by HENRY MANCINI
Arranged by Eugénie Rocherolle

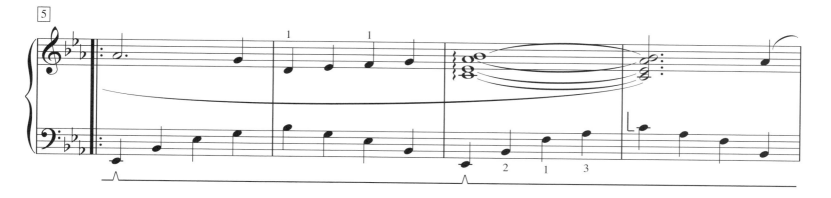

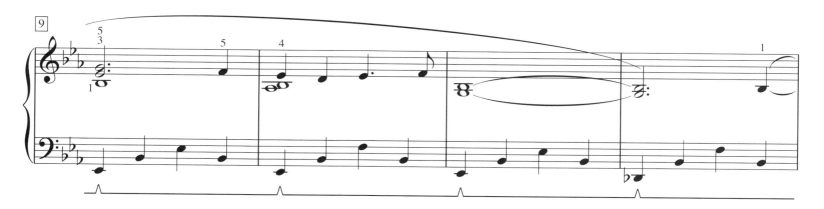

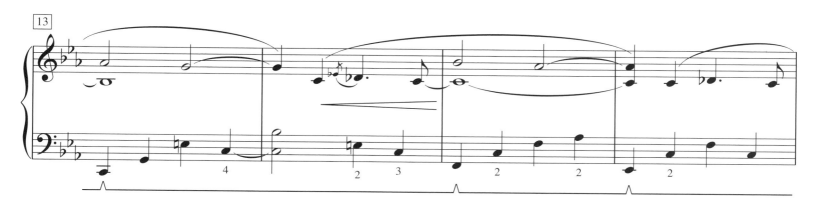

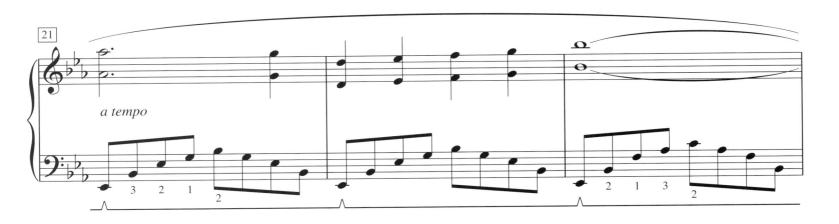

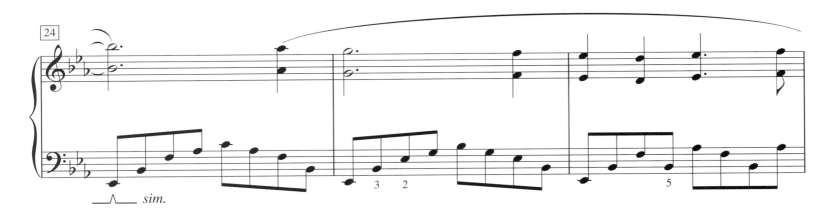

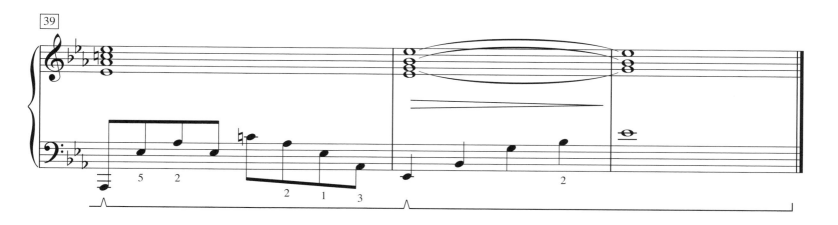

INSPECTOR CLOUSEAU THEME

By HENRY MANCINI
Arranged by Eugénie Rocherolle

Lively (♩ = 160)

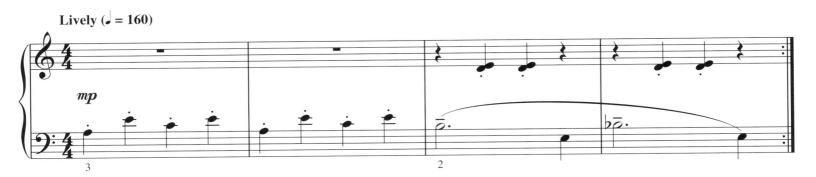

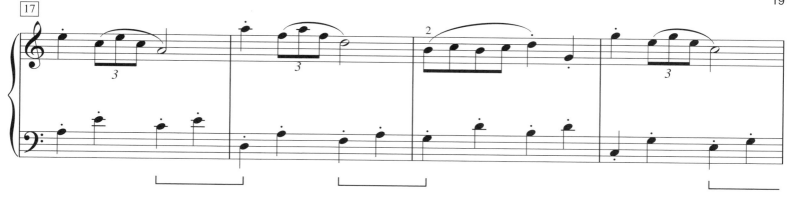

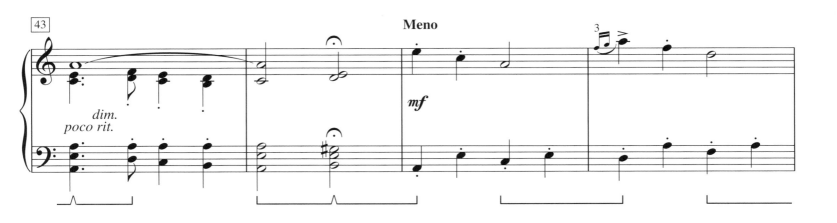

Tempo primo

IT HAD BETTER BE TONIGHT

Music by HENRY MANCINI
English Lyrics by JOHNNY MERCER
Italian Lyrics by FRANCO MIGLIACCI
Arranged by Eugénie Rocherolle

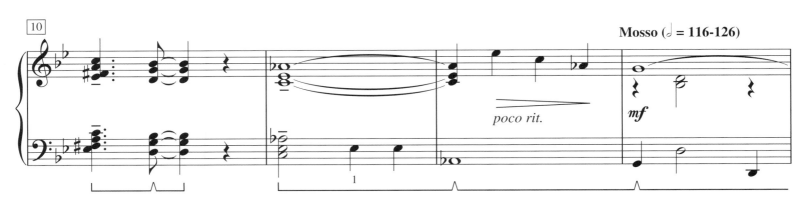

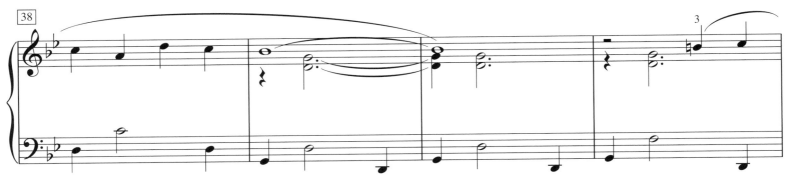

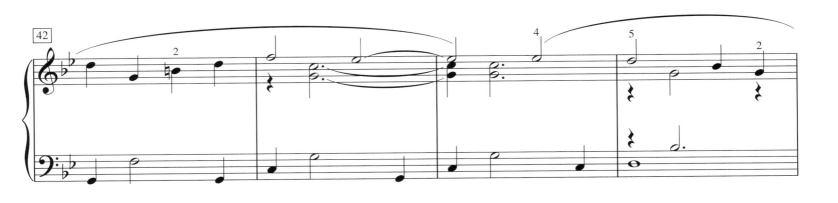

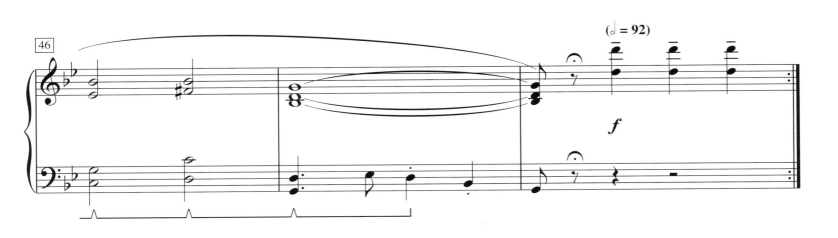

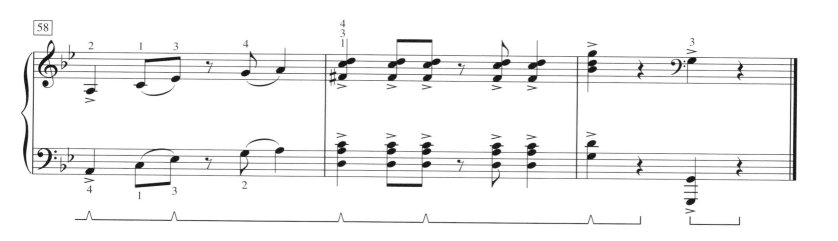

MOMENT TO MOMENT

By HENRY MANCINI
Arranged by Eugénie Rocherolle

Slowly, tenderly (♩ = 56)

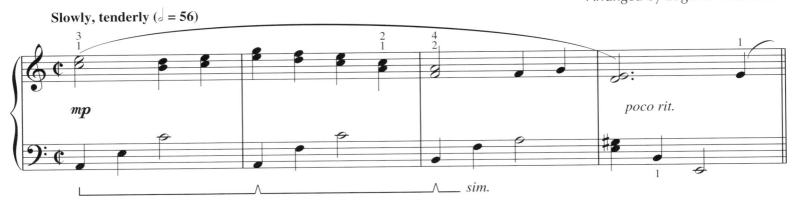

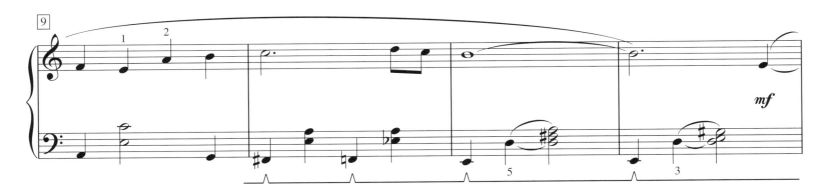

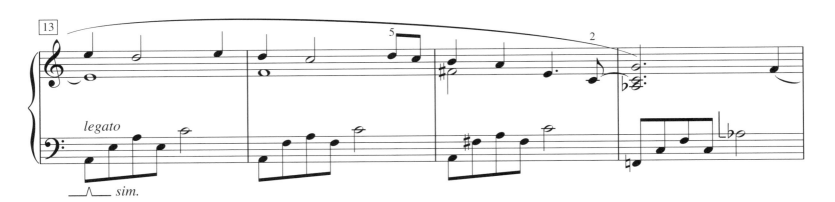

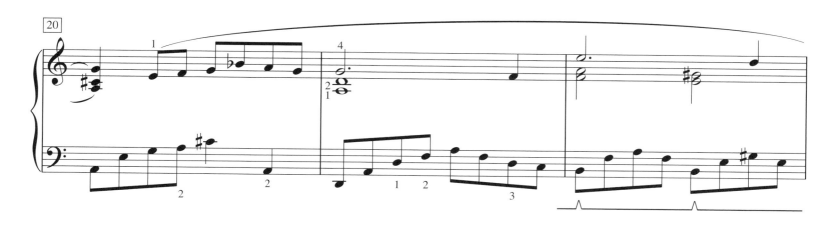

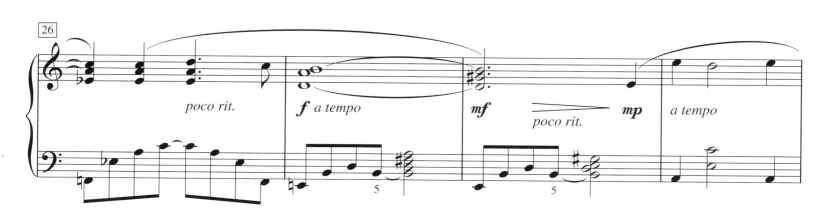

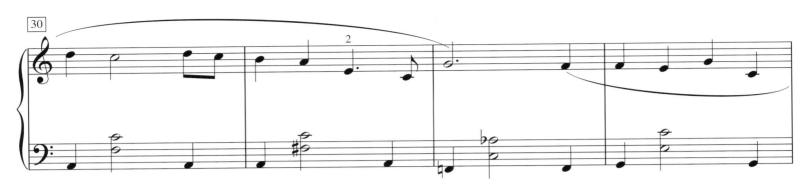

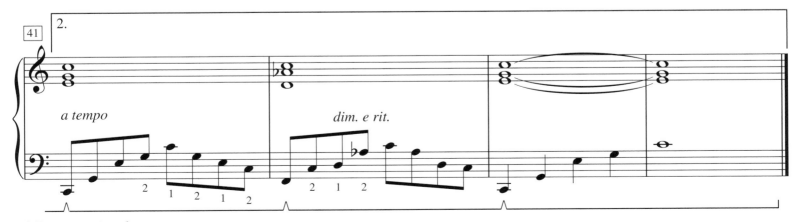

Repeat optional

MOON RIVER

from the Paramount Picture BREAKFAST AT TIFFANY'S

Words by JOHNNY MERCER
Music by HENRY MANCINI
Arranged by Eugénie Rocherolle

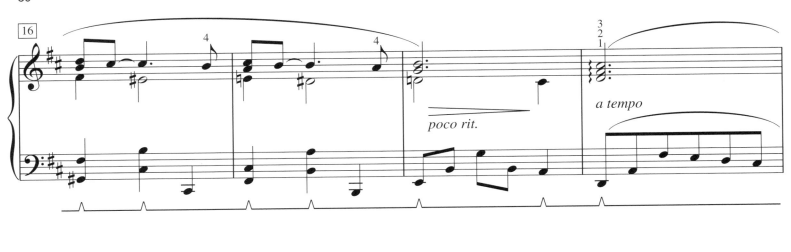

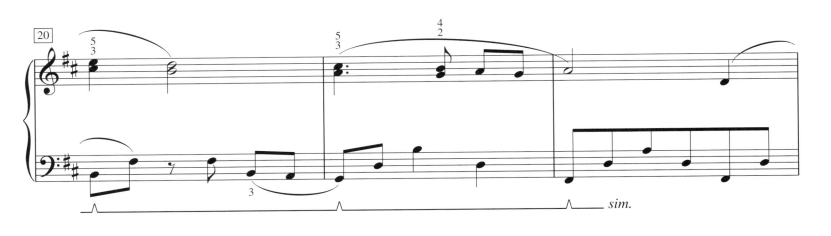

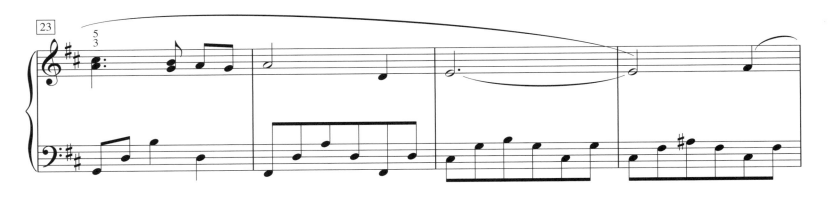

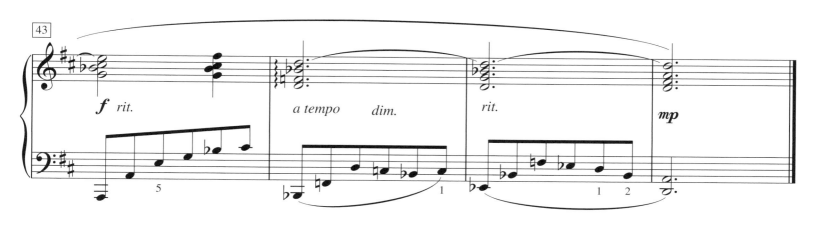

THE EUGÉNIE ROCHEROLLE SERIES

Offering both original compositions and popular arrangements, these stunning collections are ideal for intermediate-level pianists! Each book includes a companion CD with recordings performed by Ms. Rocherolle.

  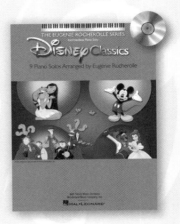 

Candlelight Christmas
Eight traditional carols: Away in a Manger • Coventry Carol • Joseph Dearest, Joseph Mine • O Holy Night (duet) • O Little Town of Bethlehem • Silent Night • The Sleep of the Infant Jesus • What Child Is This?
00311808..$14.99

Christmas Together
Six intermediate level piano duet arrangements: Blue Christmas • The Christmas Song (Chestnuts Roasting on an Open Fire) • Rudolph the Red-Nosed Reindeer • Santa Baby • Up on the Housetop • We Wish You a Merry Christmas.
00102838 ....$14.99

Classic Jazz Standards
Ten beloved tunes: Blue Skies • Georgia on My Mind • Isn't It Romantic? • Lazy River • The Nearness of You • On the Sunny Side of the Street • Stardust • Stormy Weather • and more.
00311424 ....$12.95

Continental Suite
Enjoy the wonders of Europe through these six original piano solos at the intermediate level: Belgian Lace • In Old Vienna • La Piazza • Les Avenues De Paris • Oktoberfest • Rondo Capichio.
00312111 ....$12.99

Disney Classics
Nine classic Disney songs as intermediate piano solos: Beauty and the Beast • Bibbidi-Bobbidi-Boo • Chim Chim Cher-ee • A Dream Is a Wish Your Heart Makes • It's a Small World • Mickey Mouse March • Supercalifragilisticexpialidocious • A Whole New World • Zip-A-Dee-Doo-Dah.
00312272 ....$14.99

It's Me, O Lord
Nine traditional spirituals: Deep River • It's Me, O Lord • Nobody Knows De Trouble I See • Swing Low, Sweet Chariot • and more.
00311368..$12.95

On the Jazzy Side
Six delightful jazz piano solos composed by Rocherolle, with her recordings of each on the enclosed CD! Songs: High Five! • Jubilation! • Prime Time • Small Talk • Small Town Blues • Travelin' Light.
00311982..$12.99

Recuerdos Hispanicos
Seven original solos: Brisas Isleñas (Island Breezes) • Dia de Fiesta (Holiday) • Un Amor Quebrado (A Lost Love) • Resonancias de España (Echoes of Spain) • Niña Bonita (Pretty Girl) • Fantasia del Mambo (Mambo Fantasy) • Cuentos del Matador (Tales of the Matador).
00311369..$12.95

Rodgers & Hammerstein Selected Favorites
Exquisite, intermediate-level piano solo arrangements of eight favorites from these beloved composers: Climb Ev'ry Mountain • Do-Re-Mi • If I Loved You • Oklahoma • Shall We Dance? • Some Enchanted Evening • There Is Nothin' like a Dame • You'll Never Walk Alone. Includes a CD of Eugénie performing each song.
00311928..$14.99

Swingin' the Blues
Six blues originals: Back Street Blues • Big Shot Blues • Easy Walkin' Blues • Hometown Blues • Late Night Blues • Two-Way Blues.
00311445..$12.95

Two's Company
Eugénie Rocherolle gives us a charming and whimsical collection of five original piano duets written for the intermediate-level pianist. The CD includes a recording by Rocherolle of the duet, primo and secondo tracks allowing the performer to practice along with the CD. Duets include: Island Holiday • La Danza • Mood in Blue • Postcript • Whimsical Waltz.
00311883 ....$12.99

Valses Sentimentales
Seven original solos: Bal Masque (Masked Ball) • Jardin de Thé (Tea Garden) • Le Long du Boulevard (Along the Boulevard) • Marché aux Fleurs (Flower Market) • Nuit sans Etoiles (Night Without Stars) • Palais Royale (Royal Palace) • Promenade á Deux (Strolling Together).
00311497..$12.95

HAL•LEONARD®

www.halleonard.com

0513